HAPPY COOKING!!

Published in 2004 by Big Chef Books
www.thebigchef.com
In association with Pathfinder Paperbacks

This edition published in 2005

ISBN: 0-9550267-0-9

©Copyright 2004, Peter Osborne
peter@thebigchef.com

Cover Design and Layout – Stephen Young: latouveilhe@mac.com

Printed by Basingstoke Press

Happy Cooking!!

Peter Osborne

'The Big Chef'

Big Chef Books

Foreword

Strangely enough, I first met Peter Osborne – 'The Big Chef' – when I rushed into his kitchen during a live radio outside broadcast. What do I remember most from our first meeting? A delicious Sicilian Pasta dish!

Since then, Peter and I have become great friends and he is a regular guest on my Classic Gold radio show. He is also at the end of the telephone to regularly rescue me from disaster in my own kitchen.

So – who is The Big Chef? Peter Osborne is a larger than life character who loves to cook but also someone who loves to share his culinary secrets and prove that cooking is fun!!

This book contains a recipe for every occasion but they all have one thing in common. They are easy to follow and will help you create delicious meals bursting with flavour. Whether you want to impress friends with a dinner party or cook yourself a tasty treat at the end of a long day, keep this book where it belongs – in your kitchen.

Having already enjoyed many of the dishes, may I recommend:–

Page 21 – Stilton and Walnut Salad
Page 55 – Garlic Roasted Chicken
Page 120 – Hot Peaches with Honey and Mascarpone

I wish you many happy meals with this book and remember to listen out for more from 'The Big Chef' on Classic Gold. Monday – Friday between 09-00 & 12-00.

Enjoy!

Graham Rogers

Dedication

To the two girls in my life.
My wonderful wife Anna-Marie, and our lovely little girl,
Amelia.
For all their love, help and support and inspiration, not only in
this project but always.

I would also like to thank my friend Graham Rogers from
Classic Gold, and indeed all my friends who helped in the
research of this book – that is – I cooked, they ate!!!!

Very special thanks to Harry Owen, Poet Laureate of Cheshire,
for the verses.

Contents

Soups 11

Starters, Snacks and Light Meals 19

Fish 39

Poultry 51

Beef, Lamb and Pork 67

Vegetarian 83

Vegetable and Potato Dishes 95

Puddings 103

Kids' Corner 123

Index 128

SOUPS

Brother of a broth or a consommé,
a meal on its own or a brisk entrée;
sieved, served ungarnished as a rich purée –
never underestimate this Soup of the Day.

Broccoli & Cheese Soup

Time to prepare – 5 minutes
Time to cook – 30 minutes
Serves – 4

225g broccoli
1 tablespoon sunflower oil
1 leek, thinly sliced
175g potatoes, diced
Salt and Freshly ground black pepper
500ml chicken stock
150ml dry white wine
115g grated cheddar cheese

Cut the stems from broccoli florets and cut into $^1/_2$-inch pieces. Heat the oil in a pan. Add the leek, potatoes and broccoli and cook, stirring occasionally, for 5 minutes. Season with salt and pepper, and then add the stock and white wine and bring to a boil. Simmer for 20 minutes, or until vegetables are tender.

Purée in a blender or food processor and return to pan. Add cheese, reserving a little for garnish, and cook over low heat, stirring, until cheese is thoroughly melted into soup. Garnish with reserved cheese and serve.

Note: Do not allow soup to boil after you add cheese or it will become stringy.

Tuscan Bean Soup

From the leaning tower, Chianti hills,
a leguminous Uffizi fills
your jaded palate's window sills.

Time to prepare – 10 minutes
Time to cook – 40 minutes
Serves – 4

1 tablespoon olive oil
1 bunch of spring onions, chopped
2 carrots, diced
2 stalks celery, sliced
2 parsnips, diced
115g swede, diced
115g turnips, diced
2 bay leaves
1 litre chicken stock or water
55g macaroni
1 can (14oz/400g) cannellini beans, drained
Salt and freshly ground black pepper
Chopped fresh parsley, to garnish

Heat the oil in a medium sized saucepan. Add the vegetables and
bay leaves.

Cook over low heat, stirring occasionally for about 10 minutes, or
until soft. Add chicken stock or water and macaroni. Bring to a boil,
reduce heat and simmer 25 minutes. Add beans and cook 5 minutes,
to warm through.

Stir well and season with salt and pepper. Remove and discard bay
leaves. Garnish with chopped parsley and serve.

Roast Parsnip Soup

Time to prepare – 5 minutes
Time to cook – 60 minutes
Serves – 4

450g parsnips cut into chunks
1 tablespoon olive oil
Salt
Freshly ground black pepper
1 large potato, cut into chunks
1 large onion, chopped
850ml vegetable stock
2 tablespoons plain yogurt
1 large pinch of freshly grated nutmeg
Plain yogurt, to garnish
Freshly grated nutmeg, to garnish

Lay the parsnips in bottom of a large pan and then drizzle with oil and season with salt and pepper.

Cook over low heat 15 – 20 minutes, turning once, until browned all over. Add potato and onion and cook, stirring occasionally, 10 minutes. Add the stock, bring to the boil and simmer 35 minutes.

Purée soup in a blender or food processor and return to pan. Stir in yogurt, nutmeg, salt and pepper and cook over low heat to warm through. Pour into warmed soup bowls, swirl in a little yogurt, sprinkle with nutmeg and serve.

2 a.m. French Onion Soup

I have called this 2 a.m. because it was at this time of the morning- in a little Bistro in Montmatre- that I was shown how to make onion soup the French way. I was about 17 and working in Paris at the time. Happy days!

Time to prepare – 5 minutes
Time to cook – 30 minutes
Serves – 4

50g beef dripping
450g large onions – sliced very thickly
25g brown sugar
25g plain flour
900ml beef stock
Salt and freshly ground pepper
Optional:-
French bread
Gruyere cheese, grated
Mustard – preferably Dijon

Peel and slice onions thickly and cook slowly in the butter until soft, but not brown. Then turn up the heat, add sugar and cook until the onions are just starting to caramelize. Stir in the flour, and cook for two minutes, add the stock and stir until bubbling. Simmer for 20 – 30 minutes, and then check seasoning.

You can serve at this stage, adding a hint of brandy to the soup before serving!!!!

Option:- Slice the bread, and toast one side. Spread mustard on untoasted side and sprinkle on cheese. Brown under the grill, and place a slice on each bowl of soup before serving.

Tomato and Red Pepper Soup

Time to prepare – 5 minutes
Time to cook – 20 minutes
Serves – 4

8 medium-size tomatoes
60g butter
1 medium-size onion, finely chopped
1 red pepper – chopped
450ml chicken stock
1 pinch saffron
1 pinch chilli powder
Salt
Fresh parsley, if desired

Put the tomatoes into a bowl and cover with boiling water for 1 minute and then drain. Cover with cold water 1 minute and drain again. Remove and discard skins and chop tomatoes. In a large saucepan, melt butter. Add onion. Cook until beginning to soften. Add tomatoes and chopped red pepper. Add stock and saffron. Bring to a boil; reduce heat. Cover; simmer for about ten minutes Stir in chilli powder and salt to taste. Garnish with parsley, if desired.

Quick Tomato and Red Pepper Soup

1 can chopped tomatoes
1 red pepper – deseeded and chopped roughly
1 pint Chicken or vegetable stock for vegetarian option
A little cream for decoration – optional

Put tomatoes into saucepan and add the red pepper. Then add the stock and bring to the boil, simmer for 5 minutes. Then liquidize until smooth and serve with a swirl of cream if you want to be naughty!!!!!!

Pear and Watercress Soup with Blue Cheese Croutons

Time to prepare – 10 minutes
Time to cook – 25 minutes
Serves – 4

1 bunch Watercress
5 pears sliced
1 litre chicken stock
Salt and pepper to taste
150ml double cream
Juice of a lime
For the croutons
25g butter
30ml olive oil
250g cubed bread (slightly stale)
150g Stilton Cheese (chopped)

Place about $^3/_4$ of the watercress into a saucepan, together with the stock and a little seasoning and simmer for about 15 minutes.

Then place the remaining watercress together with the mixture into a food processor and blend until smooth.

Put the mixture back into the saucepan, add the cream and lime juice and stir thoroughly. Reheat the soup gently and stir often.

To make the croutons, melt the oil and butter in a frying pan and then fry the bread cubes until brown. Drain on absorbent kitchen paper. Place the cubes onto a heat proof dish and sprinkle the cheese on top, heat under a hot grill until bubbling.

Serve the soup into bowls and divide the croutons and place on top of the soup.

Starters, Snacks and Light Meals

Zeitgeist:
light bite Delightgeist.

Notes

Stilton and Walnut Salad

Strong, rich and English, the stuff of ballad
– enjoy this aristocratic salad.

Time to prepare – 15 minutes
Serves – 4

2 tablespoons extra virgin olive oil
2 tablespoons walnut oil
1 tablespoon white wine vinegar

For the salad

100g mixed baby leaf salad
250g stilton, sliced
12 croutons
50g of walnuts, chopped

Mix together the extra virgin and walnut oils with the white wine vinegar and set aside. Place the salad mixture in a large bowl and pour over the dressing, mix thoroughly. To serve, divide the salad between four plates, place a few slices of stilton on top and scatter the croutons and walnuts.

Easy Peasy Spanish Omelette

¿Tienes hambre? ¡Esta tortilla
de huevos, patatas y cebollas
es un poema bonito!

Time to prepare – 2 minutes
Time to cook – 16 minutes
Serves – 2

2 tablespoons olive oil
1 onion, thinly sliced
350g potatoes, diced
1 red bell pepper, thinly sliced
1 green bell pepper, thinly sliced
6 eggs, beaten
1 tablespoon chopped fresh parsley
Salt
Freshly ground pepper

Heat oil in a shallow flameproof casserole dish. Add onion and potatoes and cook, stirring occasionally, 6 to 8 minutes, or until potatoes are tender. Stir in bell peppers and cook 2 or 3 minutes. Beat together eggs, parsley, salt and pepper and pour into dish. Cook over a low heat for 3 or 4 minutes, or until the eggs have set on the bottom. Preheat grill.

Put omelette under grill and cook for 5 or 6 minutes, or until eggs have set. Cut into wedges and serve hot or cold.

Baby Leaf Salad with Wild Mushrooms and Chicken

Time to prepare – 15 minutes
Serves – 4 as a starter, 2 as a light lunch

1-2 tablespoons of olive oil
2 chicken breasts, pan fried and cut into strips
100g wild mushrooms, sliced
1 garlic clove, finely chopped
2 tablespoons chopped parsley
1 slice of day old bread, cut into small cubes with crust removed

For the salad

4 handfuls mixed salad leaves, baby spinach, rocket etc
3 tablespoons balsamic vinegar
3 tablespoons fresh orange juice

Heat the oil in a frying pan and add the mushrooms, garlic and parsley and fry until the juices have evaporated and the mushrooms are lightly caramelised at the edges. Remove them from the pan leaving the oil behind. Re-heat the pan and fry the bread, adding more oil if necessary. To make the salad, in a large bowl pile the leaves and add the balsamic vinegar and orange juice and toss. Add the mushrooms, chicken and crisp bread cubes. Serve immediately before the salad leaves wilt.

Great with lovely crusty bread!!

Is it Pizza or is it an Omelette?

Time to prepare – 3 minutes
Time to cook – 6 minutes
Serves – 1

3 Eggs
1 teaspoon Butter
1 plum tomato, thinly sliced
1 teaspoon Basil, fresh, chopped
2 Tablespoons Italian-style sausage, cooked and cubed
2 ounces Mozzarella, grated

Pre-heat the grill. Melt the butter in a small non-stick frying pan. Lightly beat the eggs and add to the frying pan. Move eggs frequently until firm. Turn omelette over and remove from the heat. Top with the tomatoes, basil, sausage, and cheese. Place under grill until cheese has melted. Serve immediately.

Notes

Seafood Soufflé Omelette

Time to prepare – 2 minutes
Time to cook – 5 minutes
Serves – 2

    3 eggs, separated
    Salt
    Pepper
    30g butter
    125g peeled, de-veined cooked prawns
    1 tablespoon lemon juice
    1 teaspoon chilli sauce
    Lemon slices
    Fennel or dill sprigs

Preheat grill.

In a medium-size bowl, beat egg yolks, salt and pepper. In another bowl, beat egg whites until stiff. Fold into yolks. Put a 7-inch omelette pan or small frying pan over low heat to become thoroughly hot. Add half the butter. When butter is sizzling but not brown, pour in eggs and cook until base is golden-brown, 2 to 3 minutes.

While omelette is cooking, preheat grill and prepare filling. Heat the remaining butter in a small frying pan. Add prawns, lemon juice and chilli sauce and heat through. Transfer omelette to grill until lightly browned, about 30 seconds. Spoon the filling over half the omelette. Fold over, cut in half and garnish with lemon and herb sprig.

Serve immediately.

Brie and Spiced Pear Tartlets

Time to prepare – 10 minutes
Time to cook – 15-20 minutes
Serves – 4

> 80g of butter
> 200 gm pack of filo pastry
> 1 can of pears in natural juice, drained, dried and chopped
> 300g of firm Brie
> Half a teaspoon of all spice
> A tablespoon of chopped fresh chives

Pre-heat oven to 200c/gas 6 with a flat baking sheet inside (this helps to crisp the base of the tarts).

Melt butter over a gentle heat, place one sheet of filo pastry onto a board and brush both sides of the filo with butter. Fold over until you have a 3 inch square, and then push into one of the cups of a Yorkshire pudding tin, tucking the edges inside so that you have a round tart. Repeat with the other sheets, brushing each side with butter as you go. Fill each pastry case with an equal amount of pear, brie and a pinch of all spice. Stand on a pre- heated baking sheet and bake for 15-20 minutes until golden. Scatter with chives just before serving.

Mussels in White Wine

Time to prepare – 5 minutes
Time to cook – 10 minutes
Serves – 4

  1 tablespoon olive oil
  1 small onion, finely chopped
  2 plum tomatoes, peeled, seeded, chopped
  1 pinch chilli powder
  500ml dry white wine
  1^1/$_3$ kg mussels, scrubbed, trimmed
  Salt
  Freshly ground black pepper
  1 tablespoon chopped fresh flat-leaf parsley

Heat the oil in a flameproof casserole dish. Add onion and cook over a low heat, stirring occasionally, 5 minutes, or until soft. Add tomatoes, chilli powder and white wine.

Bring to the boil. Add mussels, cover tightly and cook over a high heat, shaking the dish occasionally, 3 or 4 minutes, or until the mussels open. Discard any mussels that remain closed.
Season with salt and pepper, sprinkle with parsley and serve.

Note: Before cooking mussels, discard any that are open and do not close when tapped sharply.

Smoked Salmon and Prawn Gateaux with Chive Oil

Time to prepare – 15 minutes plus chilling
Serves – 4

100g salmon fillet
4 slices smoked salmon
200g Philadelphia Cheese
100g prawns, chopped
1 shallot, finely chopped and blanched
6 chives, chopped
10 green peppercorns, finely chopped
$^1/_2$ clove garlic, crushed (optional)
A good squeeze of lemon juice
Salt and freshly ground black pepper
Crème Fraiche or Soured cream, 12 whole chives and salad
leaves to serve

For the chive oil
75ml extra virgin olive oil
2 packs fresh chives

Poach the salmon in the fish stock for 8 – 10 minutes then chill,
skin and flake the fresh salmon. In a bowl mix together the
Philadelphia cheese, chopped prawns, shallot, coriander, peppercorns
and garlic, if using, then add the poached salmon. Check the
seasoning and add lemon juice, if needed.

*The dish needs to be slightly over seasoned at this stage as the chilling
process tends to dull the taste of the seasoning.*

Lay one circle of salmon in the bottom of a ring. Spoon mixture
on top and flatten. Lay circle of salmon on top and shape flat and

then refrigerate for at least two hours. For the chive oil, place the oil and chives in a food processor and liquidise for 1 min.

Season and put through a fine sieve.

Put a few salad leaves onto the side of the plate and drizzle the oil around. Place the gateau in the centre of the plate. Finally place 3-4 whole chives on top of the gateaux.

Notes

Cucumber, Dill and Cheese mousse with Ruby grapefruit and Smoked Salmon

Green, white, deep red and pink,
fresh, sharp, smooth as a wink –
sophisticated mousse, I think . . .

Time to prepare – 20 minutes plus chilling time
Serves – 4

¹/₂ cucumber, grated
¹/₂ x 5ml spoon salt
85g goats' cheese
250g fromage frais
20g fresh dill – chopped
Few drops Tabasco sauce
2 x 5ml spoons powdered gelatine
2 ruby or pink grapefruit
Salt and freshly ground pepper

Mix together the cucumber and salt and place in a sieve over a bowl whilst you prepare the rest of the ingredients.

Beat the goats cheese in a bowl then beat in the fromage frais until it is smooth. Stir in the chopped dill and Tabasco sauce.

Squeeze the excess moisture from the cucumber – you should have about four tablespoons – into a small pan. Sprinkle the gelatine over the top of the juices. Beat the cucumber into the cheese and dill mixture.

Dissolve the gelatine, stirring over a very gentle heat. Remove the pan from the heat and add a spoonful of the cheese mixture to the liquid, then beat this into the bulk of the mixture. Check for seasoning – remember to season generously as the flavour is slightly inhibited when food is served cold.

Transfer to 4 small dishes or moulds, cover with cling film and chill until set which should be a minimum of two hours, but they may be left for 1 to 2 days in the fridge. To serve, carefully unmould the mousses onto individual plates. Using a small serrated knife, remove the skin and pith from the grapefruit and carefully cut the segments from the membrane, place around mould, together with the smoked salmon. Garnish the mousses with reserved sprigs of dill

Notes

Fishy Parcels

Time to prepare – 10 minutes
Time to cook – 25 minutes
Serves – 4

> 4 firm white fish fillets, skinned
> 1 tomato, cut into 4 slices
> 1 tablespoon olive oil
> 1 onion, sliced
> 2 teaspoons grated lemon rind
> 1 tablespoon chopped fresh parsley
> 8 black olives, pitted and chopped
> 250g puff pastry
> 1 egg, beaten

Heat the oil in a frying pan and when hot, add the onion. Cook, stirring, for 5 minutes until soft but not brown.

Take the cooked onion out of the pan, put into a bowl and add the lemon rind, parsley and olives

Cut each fish fillet in half, crossways. Top each piece of fish with some of the onion mixture, a slice of tomato, then another piece of fish, to make a stack.

Preheat oven to 180c/gas 5

Roll out pastry to 5mm thick. Cut out four large squares. Place a fish stack in the centre of each. Completely wrap with pastry.

Place on a lightly greased baking tray. Cut two vents in the top of each parcel. Brush with egg and bake for 5 minutes.

Reduce oven temperature to 160c/gas 4 and bake for 15 minutes longer or until pastry is golden.

Serving suggestions: Serve with a Green Salad or Tomato and Basil Salad.

King Prawns Flamed in Pernod with Creamy Tarragon Sauce

Time to prepare – 5 minutes
Time to cook – 6 minters
Serves – 4

50g butter
1 tablespoon finely chopped garlic
1 tablespoon finely chopped shallots
24 uncooked king prawns
2 tablespoons Pernod
125ml Double cream
1 tablespoon finely chopped tarragon
Salt and pepper
4 sprigs tarragon

In a large sauté pan, heat the butter over medium-high heat. Add the garlic, shallots, and prawns, and cook for 2 minutes. Remove the pan from the heat and add the Pernod. Return the pan to the heat and carefully flambé. Add the cream and tarragon and season with salt and pepper. Cook for 2 more minutes to reduce slightly. Garnish each serving with a tarragon leaf.

Creamy Wild Mushrooms on Hot Toasted Granary

Delicious in its creamy sauce:
tempestuous Agaricus!

Time to prepare -3 minutes
Time to cook – 6 minutes
Serves – 2

75g butter
Clove of garlic, peeled and finely chopped
350g assorted wild mushrooms
A splash of white wine
A little double cream
1 tablespoon of freshly chopped parsley
2 teaspoons of freshly chopped chives
Salt and pepper to taste
2 thick slices of granary bread

Melt the butter in a frying pan and then add the garlic. Cook gently for about 30 seconds and then add the mushrooms. Fry gently for about 3-4 minutes. Then add the wine to the pan and cook for a minute.

Then put the double cream and herbs into the pan and simmer gently. Check seasoning.

Toast the bread and place onto the serving plates, top with the mushrooms and a little fresh parsley.

Tarragon-Stuffed Mushrooms

Time to prepare – 10 minutes
Time to cook – 35 minutes
Serves – 4

    450g large button mushrooms
    1 tbsp. olive oil
    1 medium onion, finely minced
    1 clove garlic, finely minced
    1 rounded tsp. broken leaf tarragon
    1 tbsp. red wine vinegar
    2 tbsp. water
    1 tbsp. coarse brown Dijon style mustard
    2 tbsp. plain breadcrumbs

Preheat oven to 160c. Wipe off mushrooms, break the stems out of the mushroom caps as deeply as possible, and chop the stems into very small pieces. If there are a few mushrooms too small to stuff, chop them as well. If the mushroom caps need to be enlarged use a melon baller or small spoon and carefully enlarge the opening, adding the shavings to the minced mushroom stems. Have the onion and garlic finely minced and ready to go. In a small saucepan, heat olive oil over medium heat. When hot, add minced mushrooms and onions. Cook, stirring, about 3 minutes, until onions turn translucent and the mushrooms are giving up juice. Add garlic and heat for 2 more minutes. Add tarragon, vinegar, water, mustard, and breadcrumbs to the pan. Stir thoroughly and remove from heat. Fill mushroom caps with breadcrumb mixture. Place mushrooms in a glass baking dish and bake 30 minutes. Remove and serve immediately.

Chicken and Fruit Salad with Mango Vinaigrette

Time to prepare – 10 minutes
Time to cook – 15 minutes
Serves – 4

3 mango's peeled, stoned and sliced
12 ounces skinless, boneless chicken breast halves
$1/2$ teaspoon curry powder
$1/8$ teaspoon salt
$1/4$ teaspoon coarsely ground pepper
6 handsful torn mixed green leaves
$1/2$ med. cantaloupe melon, seeded, peeled, cut in 1-inch chunks
1 small punnet strawberries – halved or sliced
1 recipe Mango Vinaigrette (see below)
2 spring onions, thinly sliced

Pit, peel, and slice the mangoes. Keep $1/2$ of the mango for use in the vinaigrette; set remaining slices aside for salad. Rinse chicken; pat dry with kitchen roll. Stir together the curry, salt, and pepper. Rub chicken with curry mixture. Place chicken on the unheated rack of a grill pan. Grill 4 to 5 inches from the heat for 10 to 12 minutes, turning once. Cool chicken slightly; slice into $1/4$-inch strips. Arrange green leaves on individual dinner plates. Top with chicken strips, melon, strawberries, and reserved mango slices. Drizzle each salad with some of the Mango Vinaigrette. Sprinkle onion over all.

MANGO VINAIGRETTE:

In a blender container or food processor bowl, combine the remaining mango, 150cl orange juice, 3 tablespoons rice vinegar or white wine vinegar, 2 teaspoons honey, and 1 teaspoon Dijon-style mustard. Cover and blend or process until smooth. Cover and chill until serving time.

Latvian Potato Pancakes with Smoked Salmon

Here's Riga's gift to Europe's world of food,
where Atlantic salmon elevates the mood.

Time to prepare – 10 minutes
Time to cook – 10 minutes
Serves – 4

500g King Edward Potatoes
1 medium onion finely chopped
1 large egg
2 tablespoons wholemeal flour
Salt and black pepper to taste
200g smoked salmon
150ml fromage frais
A little oil for frying
Sprigs of flat leaf parsley to garnish

Preheat the oven to gas mark 4/180c. Peel and grate the potatoes and add to the finely chopped onion and put them in a sieve. Press with a wooden spoon to squeeze out as much liquid as possible and then put into a bowl. Add the egg, flour, salt and pepper and mix well.

Pour a little oil into a frying pan and heat until hot. Divide the potato mixture into eight, flatten into a small pancake and add to the pan one at a time. Fry them for about one minute then turn over and cook the other side until crisp and golden on the outside.

Remove the pancakes from the pan and place onto kitchen paper and keep warm. Cut the smoked salmon into strips. Serve each pancake topped with a spoonful of fromage frais, a few strips of salmon and garnish with parsley.

FISH

From sea, lake or river, there never was ever
a food more nutritious, more soleful, delicious
than salmon, cod, halibut and other fishes . . .

Notes

Baked Saddle of Salmon

Time to prepare – 10 minutes plus chilling
Time to cook – 45 minutes
Serves – 4

  55g butter, softened
  1 clove garlic, crushed
  Juice of ¹/₂ lemon
  2 tablespoons chopped fresh parsley
  1 saddle of salmon (1¹/₂lb/750g), filleted
  1 tablespoon of olive oil
  6 shallots, chopped
  150ml fish stock
  175ml red wine
  250ml veal stock
  Salt and freshly ground black pepper

In a small bowl, mix the butter with garlic, lemon juice and 1
tablespoon of the chopped parsley.

Spread inside of one salmon piece with butter mixture and
sandwich pieces back together. Wrap tightly in cling film and put in
freezer about 1 hour, to set. Do not freeze. Preheat oven to 200c/gas
6. Lightly oil a large piece of foil. Take the salmon out of cling film
and wrap tightly in foil. Place in a shallow ovenproof dish and bake
30 to 35 minutes. Remove from dish and keep warm.

Heat oil in a flameproof dish; add shallots and cook over low
heat, stirring, 3 minutes, or until it is soft. Add fish stock and red
wine and boil until reduced and syrupy. Add veal stock and boil to
reduce slightly. Add remaining parsley and season with salt and
pepper. Divide sauce among warmed serving plates. Slice the salmon,
place on top of sauce and serve.

Halibut with a Rich Orange Sauce

Time to prepare – 5 minutes
Time to cook – 20 minutes
Serves – 2

> 55g plain flour
> $^1/_2$ teaspoon freshly grated nutmeg
> 2 halibut steaks, about 170g each
> 25g butter
> 6 spring onions, sliced
> 175ml fresh orange juice
> 1 tablespoon Worcestershire sauce
> juice of $^1/_2$ lemon
> salt and freshly ground black pepper – to taste

Mix together flour and nutmeg and use to coat halibut.

Heat butter in a shallow frying pan. Add the spring onions to the pan and cook gently, stirring occasionally for 3 minutes, or until soft.

Add the halibut and cook over a low heat for 5 to 6 minutes on each side until just cooked. Remove from the pan with a fish slice and keep warm.

Into the pan put the orange juice, Worcestershire sauce, lemon juice, salt and pepper and boil rapidly until reduced and thickened.

Pour over fish and serve.

Sea Queen Scallops with Lemon

Time to prepare – 2 minutes
Time to cook – 6 minutes
Serves – 4

4 strands saffron
Juice of 1 lemon
1 tablespoon olive oil
8 Sea Queen Scallops, sliced
1 bunch of spring onions, sliced
1 clove garlic, crushed
Salt
Freshly ground black pepper
2 teaspoons crème fraiche
Lemon twists, to garnish

In a small bowl, soak saffron in lemon juice 1 hour. Heat oil in a
pan. Add the scallops and cook, stirring, for 2 or 3 minutes.

Remove with a slotted spoon and keep warm. Add spring onions
and garlic to dish and cook over low heat, stirring occasionally, 3
minutes, or until soft. Strain lemon juice, discarding saffron strands.
Add lemon juice to dish and stir well to incorporate all juices.

Season with salt and pepper. Remove from heat and stir in crème
fraiche. Arrange scallops on individual serving plates and top with
sauce. Garnish with lemon twists and serve.

*Note: If scallops still have their roe attached when you buy
them, you can use that in the dish, too.*

Seafood Lasagne

Time to prepare – 10 minutes
Time to cook – 60 minutes
Serves – 4

2 tablespoons olive oil
1 leek, thinly sliced
225g mushrooms, thinly sliced
225g haddock fillet, skinned, cubed
115g cooked, peeled small prawns
300g cod fillets, skinned, cubed
2 tablespoons lemon juice
Salt and freshly ground pepper
4 eggs, beaten
55g freshly grated Parmesan cheese
500ml plain yoghurt
6 wide fresh lasagne sheets
225g mozzarella cheese, sliced

Heat oil in a flameproof casserole dish and add leek and mushrooms. Cook over low heat 10 minutes, stirring occasionally, until soft. Add haddock, prawns, cod, lemon juice, salt and pepper and cook, stirring, 5 minutes. Preheat oven to gas 4/180c. Mix together eggs, Parmesan cheese and yoghurt. Stir two-thirds of egg mixture into fish mixture. Remove two-thirds of fish mixture from dish.

Cover fish mixture in dish with 2 lasagne sheets. Cover them with half of remaining fish mixture, then 2 more lasagne sheets. Spread remaining fish mixture over lasagne sheets Cover with remaining sheets and pour reserved egg mixture over top. Cover with cheese and bake 40 to 50 minutes, or until topping is golden and pasta is tender. Serve.

Baked Cod Italienne

Time to prepare – 5 minutes
Time to cook – 35 minutes
Serves – 4

    30g butter
    125g sliced mushrooms
    1 jar passata
    4 cod steaks, about 155g each or other white fish
    Salt and freshly ground pepper
    125g pasta shells
    8 black olives

Preheat oven to 190c/gas 5. In a medium-size saucepan, melt butter. Add mushrooms; cook gently until soft. Stir in the passata.

Put fish into a buttered 2-quart oblong baking dish. Season with salt and pepper. Pour tomato and mushroom sauce over fish. Cover dish with foil; bake about 25 minutes or until fish is opaque when tested with a fork.

Meanwhile, cook pasta until just tender to the bite. About 5 minutes before fish has finished cooking, arrange pasta around fish, spooning some of sauce over pasta. Garnish with olives and serve.

Scampi Olé

Time to prepare – 10 minutes
Time to cook – 35 minutes
Serves – 4

4 ripe tomatoes	250ml water
1 Spanish onion	salt and freshly ground pepper
2 courgettes	to taste
1 red pepper, cored, seeded	500g raw, peeled scampi
60ml olive oil	45g fresh white breadcrumbs
1 clove garlic, crushed	3 teaspoons chopped
15g plain flour	marjoram
60ml dry white wine	125g mozzarella cheese
1 tablespoon tomato puree	Sprigs of marjoram, to garnish

Preheat oven to 375F (190c). Put tomatoes in a bowl, cover with boiling water and leave for 30 seconds; drain and peel away skins, then chop coarsely. Quarter and thinly slice onion. Cut courgettes into $1/4$-inch slices. Cut red pepper into fairly thin strips.

In a saucepan, heat 3 tablespoons oil, add garlic, onion, courgettes and red pepper and cook gently for 3 minutes.

Stir in flour and cook for 1 minute. Add wine, tomato purée and 125ml water. Season with salt and pepper and cook over low heat for 5 minutes, stirring occasionally. Add tomatoes and mix well. Divide mixture between 4 individual ovenproof dishes. Top with the scampi.

Heat the remaining oil in a pan. Remove from heat and stir in bread crumbs and marjoram; mix well. Sprinkle over mixture in dishes. Chop mozzarella cheese and sprinkle on top. Cook in the oven for 30 minutes or until the topping is golden and the scampi is cooked. Serve hot, garnished with sprigs of marjoram.

Fish Gratins

A day without sunshine?
A tree without wood?
No fish out of water
ever tasted this good!

Time to prepare – 5 minutes
Time to cook – 6 minutes
Serves – 4

> $^1/_2$ teaspoon Dijon mustard
> 1 tablespoon lemon juice
> 1 tablespoon olive oil
> 1 pinch of freshly grated nutmeg
> Salt and freshly ground pepper
> 4 cod or haddock steaks, about 150g each
> 5g finely shredded sharp cheddar cheese
> 45g freshly grated Parmesan cheese
> 2 tablespoons fine fresh bread crumbs
> Paprika
> Basil sprigs to garnish

Preheat grill. In a small bowl, beat together mustard and lemon juice using a fork, then gradually beat in oil. Add nutmeg and season with salt and pepper. Place fish in a pan. Brush 1 side of each fish with mustard mixture, then grill, coated sides up, 2 minutes. Turn fish over, brush tops with mustard mixture, and grill 2 minutes longer.

Cover fish with Cheddar cheese. Mix together Parmesan cheese and bread crumbs, then sprinkle evenly over fish. Season generously with pepper. Grill until the top is golden and bubbling.

Lightly sprinkle with paprika. Serve garnished with sprigs of basil.

Monkfish on Ratatouille

Meditate once more in thoughts serene,
an angler on rafts of red and green.

Time to prepare – 10 minutes
Time to cook – 90 minutes
Serves – 4

2 aubergines, halved lengthways
3 courgettes, sliced
Salt and freshly ground black pepper to taste
2 monkfish tails about 2.5 lbs.
6 cloves garlic
75ml olive oil
1 Spanish onion, very thinly sliced
2 large red bell peppers, thinly sliced
4 large tomatoes, peeled, seeded, chopped
Leaves from a few sprigs of thyme
Marjoram
Oregano
About 2 tablespoons chopped parsley
About 2 tablespoons torn basil

Cut aubergines into 1-inch slices. Into a colander, put aubergine and courgettes slices. Sprinkle with salt and let stand 1 hour. Rinse well, then pat dry with kitchen roll.

Meanwhile, remove fine skin from monkfish and cut slits in flesh. Cut 3 garlic cloves into thin slivers, then insert in slits. Season with salt and pepper and set aside. Chop remaining garlic. In a heavy large saucepan, heat 2 tablespoons oil. Add aubergine slices and sauté a few minutes. Add 1 tablespoon oil and the onion and

48

chopped garlic and sauté a few minutes. Add bell peppers and cook 1 minute, stirring occasionally.

Add 2 more tablespoons oil and courgettes. Cook, stirring occasionally, a few minutes, then add the tomatoes. Snip in herb leaves and season with salt and pepper. Cover and simmer 30 to 40 minutes, stirring occasionally, or until fairly dry.

Meanwhile, preheat oven to 200c/gas 6.

Stir parsley into ratatouille and then turn ratatouille into a baking dish.

Lay monkfish on top and bake for about 30 minutes, turning the fish occasionally, or until the fish flakes. Sprinkle with basil just before end of cooking.

Notes

Fillets of Sole with Mint & Cucumber

Time to prepare – 5 minutes and 30 minutes draining
Time to cook – 10 minutes
Serves – 4

Cucumber, halved lengthways, seeded, cut into 5 cm strips
Salt
White pepper
4 sole fillets 180g each, skinned
1 small shallot, finely chopped
175ml fish stock
115ml medium-dry white wine
175ml crème fraiche or sour cream
5 mint leaves, torn
25g unsalted butter, diced
Mint leaves to garnish

Into a colander, place cucumber. Sprinkle with salt and let drain 30 minutes. Rinse and dry well with kitchen roll. Fold the fillets in half, skinned side in. Into a small frying pan, place folded fillets with shallot. Add stock and wine and heat until just simmering. Poach 4 to 5 minutes, and then transfer to a warm plate and cover to keep warm.

Add cucumber to poaching liquid, increase heat, and boil until liquid is reduced by three-quarters. Add crème fraiche or sour cream and boil until beginning to thicken. Add mint, salt, pepper, and juices collected on plate with fish. Simmer 3 minutes.

Remove pan from heat and gradually swirl in butter. Spoon the sauce over fish.

POULTRY

Braised, baked or roasted – what's your poussin?

Notes

Orchard Chicken

Time to prepare – 10 minutes
Time to cook – 50 minutes
Serves – 4

4 chicken breasts
150g red plums
150g dessert apples
150g conference pears
6 rashers of streaky Bacon- cut into lardons (medium strips)
A little plain flour – for coating the chicken breasts
100g chopped onion
About 1 litre chicken stock (homemade or stock cubes)
1 teaspoon crushed coriander seed
$^1/_2$ teaspoon ground cinnamon
3 stem ginger knobs – chopped
2 tablespoons ginger syrup
Lemon juice to taste

Heat a fairly large pan, place the bacon strips into the pan and cook, so that the juices start to run, stirring occasionally. Lightly flour the chicken breasts and fry with the bacon pieces, until crisp and golden.

Halve and stone the plums and then slice and core the apples and pears. Remove the chicken from the pan, then add the onion and fry until they just start to colour. Replace the chicken and cover with just enough stock to cover the chicken breasts.

Mix in the coriander, cinnamon, and chopped ginger knobs. Simmer for 20 minutes, and then add the fruit and ginger syrup. Cover and simmer gently until the chicken is tender. Add lemon juice and seasoning to taste, although you will probably find if you made the stock from cubes you will not need to add any more salt. Serve with jacket potatoes or boiled new potatoes tossed in herbs and butter!!!!!

Duck Breasts with Apples & Prunes

Time to prepare – 5 minutes
Time to cook – 75 minutes
Serves – 4

1 tablespoon olive oil
4 boneless duck breasts 115g each
2 cooking apples, peeled, cored, sliced
225g pitted prunes
550ml unsweetened apple juice
Salt and freshly ground black pepper

Preheat oven to 200c/gas 6. Heat oil in a shallow flameproof casserole dish, add duck and cook 3 or 4 minutes on each side, until browned.

Cover with the apple slices and prunes. Pour apple juice over duck and season with salt and pepper. Bring to a boil, cover with a lid or piece of foil and bake 55 – 60 minutes, or until duck is cooked through. Remove duck from dish with a slotted spoon, leaving behind apples and prunes, and keep warm.

Bring cooking juices in dish to a boil and boil 5 minutes, or until liquid has reduced and thickened. Pour the sauce, apples and prunes over duck and serve.

Garlic Roasted Chicken

Time to prepare – 5 minutes
Time to cook – 60 minutes
Serves – 4

  2 tablespoons olive oil
  6 cloves garlic, thinly sliced
  8 chicken thighs
  115g fennel, cut into wide strips
  1 carrot, cut into wide strips
  1 parsnip, cut into wide strips
  1 large potato, diced
  1 red bell pepper, diced
  1 green bell pepper, chopped

Preheat oven to 220c/gas 7.

On the hob, heat the oil in a shallow flameproof dish.
Add the garlic and cook 2 or 3 minutes. Place the chicken and
vegetables into the pan and turn to coat in the garlic oil.

Put the lid on the casserole and bake for 55 or 60 minutes, or
until juices are clear when chicken is pierced with a fork. Serve hot.

Chicken Breast stuffed with Palma Ham and Mozzarella

Time to prepare – 10 minutes
Time to cook – 25 minutes
Serves – 4

   4 Chicken Breasts – trimmed and skinned
   340g Grated Mozzarella
   6 Slices Palma Ham
   8 Basil Leaves
   Salt and freshly ground black pepper
   1 Bag of pre-washed spinach

Place each breast between cling film and baton out with either a rolling pin or the palm of your hand until flat (be gentle but firm as you don't want to damage the flesh) and season well.

In a bowl combine the mozzarella, Palma Ham and basil with a little black pepper.

Divide the mixture between the breasts – laying a thin layer from the bottom edge upwards, leaving at least a 1" (25mm) space at the top edge.

Roll up like a Swiss roll, ensuring the pressure is constant to get a solid sausage. Wrap the cling film tight, then wrap around with foil to make a solid 'cracker'. Place the chicken in a large pan of boiling water for 25 minutes, then remove and leave to rest for 5 minutes. Meanwhile make two small holes in the top of the bag of spinach and place into a microwave for 3 minutes on full power. Remove and divide between plates.

Unwrap the chicken, slice and serve on top of the spinach.

Ragout of chicken with wild mushrooms

A savour renewed, a flavour revived:
good taste in ragout is never contrived.

Time to prepare – 5 minutes
Time to cook – 20 minutes
Serves – 4

> A little olive oil
> 4 Chicken Breasts
> To make the jus:-
>> 600ml good chicken stock
>> two thyme sprigs
>> One tarragon sprig
> Mushrooms:
>> 30ml (2 tbsp.) olive oil
>> 400g wild mushrooms (e.g. chestnut, or chanterelles), cleaned and sliced
>> Watercress for decoration

Put a little extra virgin olive oil into a frying pan and heat. Season the chicken breasts with salt and freshly ground pepper, and put into the pan.

Brown the chicken breasts all over, and then add the chicken stock, thyme and tarragon, and simmer until cooked. Heat the olive oil in a frying pan; add the wild mushrooms and sauté over a high heat for 6-7 minutes until tender.

To serve, slice the chicken breasts and place on the warmed serving plate and scatter the mushrooms around. Pour over the jus and serve at once.

Chicken on the Vine

Time to prepare – 5 minutes
Time to cook – 20 minutes
Serves – 4

4 chicken breasts – halved, boned, and skinned
Salt and freshly grated nutmeg, as needed
2 tablespoons butter or margarine
1 tablespoon orange marmalade
$^1/4$ teaspoon dried tarragon
2 spring onions, thinly sliced (use part of the green)
80ml dry white wine
100g seedless grapes
4 floz whipping cream

Sprinkle chicken breasts with salt and nutmeg. In a large frying pan, heat butter over medium-high heat and brown chicken lightly. Add marmalade, tarragon, spring onion, and wine. Cover, reduce heat, and simmer 10 minutes; add grapes, cover again, and continue cooking until chicken is cooked through (about 10 minutes longer; test in the thickest part with a small kitchen knife). Using a slotted spoon, remove the chicken and grapes to a heated serving dish; keep warm. Add the cream to the liquid in season to taste. Pour sauce over chicken and serve.

Chicken Livers with Mango

Time to prepare – 5 minutes
Time to cook – 12 minutes
Serves – 4

1 tablespoon olive oil
1 small onion, chopped
350g chicken livers, trimmed
300ml low-fat fromage frais
2 teaspoons Worcestershire sauce
2 teaspoons whole-grain mustard
1 mango, sliced
Basil sprigs, to garnish

Heat the oil in a flameproof casserole dish. Add onion and cook, stirring occasionally, 5 minutes, or until soft. Add chicken livers and cook, stirring, 5 minutes.

In a small bowl, mix together fromage frais or sour cream, Worcestershire sauce and mustard. Add to chicken livers in dish.

Add mango slices and cook over low heat, stirring, 2 minutes. Garnish with basil sprigs and serve immediately.

Stuffed British Poussin with a Watercress Sauce

Time to prepare – 10 minutes
Time to cook – 50 minutes
Serves – 4

4 Poussin
Watercress sprigs, to garnish

STUFFING:
115g fresh whole-wheat breadcrumbs
55g dried apricots, chopped
1 bunch watercress, chopped
55g hazelnuts, chopped
Salt and freshly ground black pepper
1 egg yolk

WATERCRESS SAUCE:
1 onion, finely chopped
1 bunch watercress, chopped
115ml dry white wine
1 tablespoon chopped fresh tarragon
1 teaspoon lemon juice
55ml plain yogurt

Preheat oven to 200c/gas 6. To make stuffing, mix together bread crumbs, apricots, watercress, hazelnuts, salt and pepper. Stir in egg yolk. Use to stuff cavity of each bird. Place Poussin in a shallow flameproof dish and roast for 40 to 50 minutes, or until cooked through. To test, pierce thigh with a skewer: if the juices run clear, the poussin are cooked so remove from dish and keep warm.

To make watercress sauce, add onion to cooking juices in dish and cook over low heat, stirring occasionally, 5 minutes, or until soft. Add chopped watercress and stir well. Add white wine, tarragon and lemon juice and heat gently. Stir in yogurt and season with salt and pepper. Heat gently to warm through.

Pour sauce on to warmed serving plates and place Poussin on top. Garnish with watercress and serve.

Notes

Thai Chicken

Time to prepare – 5 minutes
Time to cook – 15 minutes
Serves – 4

2 teaspoons olive oil
1 fresh red chilli, cored, seeded, finely chopped
1 piece fresh ginger (1-inch/2^1/2cm), peeled, grated
1 teaspoon lemon grass paste
225g chanterelle mushrooms
1^1/2 teaspoons Thai red curry paste
250ml coconut milk
1 tablespoon light soy sauce
350g skinless, boneless chicken breast, cubed
Coriander sprigs, chopped coriander, to garnish

Heat oil in a flameproof casserole dish. Add chilli, ginger, lemon grass paste and mushrooms and stir-fry 2 or 3 minutes.

Add curry paste and stir-fry for a further minute. Add the coconut milk and soy sauce and bring to a boil.

Add chicken and simmer 10 minutes, or until chicken is tender and cooked through. Garnish with coriander sprigs and chopped coriander and serve.

Note: If lemon grass paste is not available, replace it with 1 teaspoon chopped fresh lemon grass, or ^{1}/2 teaspoon dried.

Turkey Milanese

Time to prepare – 5 minutes
Time to cook – 50 minutes
Serves – 4

　1 egg, beaten
　115g fresh white bread crumbs
　Grated rind of 1 lemon
　Juice of 1 lemon
　Salt and freshly ground black pepper
　4 turkey breast fillets (4oz/115g each), pounded until thin
　25g butter
　2 tablespoons olive oil
　350g courgettes, sliced
　2 teaspoons chopped fresh tarragon
　Lemon wedges, to serve

Place egg in a shallow bowl. Mix together bread crumbs, lemon rind, salt and pepper and put on a large plate. Dip turkey in egg and then bread crumbs.

Preheat oven to 200c/gas 6. Heat butter and oil in a shallow flameproof casserole dish. Add the turkey and cook 3 minutes on each side, until crisp and golden. Add courgettes and tarragon.

Sprinkle with lemon juice and season with pepper. Cover and bake for 35 to 40 minutes. Serve with lemon wedges.

Lemon Chicken Couscous

The spirit of North Africa
tastes of dreams –
so eat!

Time to prepare – 10 minutes
Time to cook – 80 minutes
Serves 4

2 tablespoons olive oil
2 red onions cut into wedges
2 red peppers, deseeded and cut into chunks
2 boneless chicken breasts, halved
4 chicken drumsticks
4 chicken thighs
100gms black olives
600ml vegetable stock
Juice of a lemon
3 tablespoons freshly chopped parsley

For the couscous
300gms couscous
Grated rind of 2 lemons
Hot vegetable stock to cover

Pre heat the oven to 190c/gas 5. Heat the oil in a large flame proof casserole, add the onions, peppers and cook until golden then remove. Add the chicken pieces and cook until golden. Meanwhile, tip the couscous into a bowl with the grated lemon rind and pour over enough stock to cover. Leave to stand for 5 minutes while the chicken browns. Remove the chicken from the pan, add the couscous, the onions, and peppers and then place the chicken back on top. Pour over the vegetable stock, cover and cook for 45 minutes or until the chicken pieces are completely cooked. During the cooking time, if the casserole looks dry, top up with a little more hot stock. Serve, seasoned with lemon juice and parsley sprinkled over.

Notes

Beef, Lamb and Pork

A cut above the rest is Caesar's cook —
yond casserole has a lean and hungry look!

Notes

The Big Chef's Hot Pot

Time to prepare – 10 minutes
Time to cook 2 hours, but the longer the better
Serves – 4

> 500g middle or best end lamb
> Salt and Pepper to taste
> 2 carrots
> 1 small turnip
> 1 small swede
> 2 sliced leeks
> 1 kilo peeled and sliced potatoes
> 2 lamb stock cubes made up in $1/2$ litre water
> A little beef dripping

Cut meat into neat pieces and dust with pepper and salt.
Put a layer of sliced potatoes on the bottom of a casserole dish.
Then place alternate layers of meat and vegetables a bit like making a lasagne.

Add extra seasonings if wanted. Finish with a layer of thickly sliced potatoes, overlapping. Pour in about $1/2$ litre of lamb stock – sufficient to come about one-third of the way up the casserole – and cover the top of the potatoes with little dabs of dripping.

Cover casserole and put into oven at 140c/gas 3 for about 2 hours. For the last half an hour uncover the casserole, raise the oven to 180c/gas 5 and brown the top layer of potatoes.

Beef Goulash with Chilli

Time to prepare – 10 minutes
Time to cook – 90 minutes
Serves – 4

 2 tablespoons olive oil
 1 onion, sliced
 1 clove garlic, crushed
 2 teaspoons paprika
 700g lean braising steak, cubed
 1 pinch caraway seeds
 2 bay leaves
 1 tablespoon balsamic vinegar
 450ml beef stock
 Salt and freshly ground black pepper
 700g potatoes, diced
 2 green bell peppers, sliced
 1 fresh green chilli, cored, seeded, sliced
 1 can (14oz 400g) chopped tomatoes
 2 tablespoons tomato paste

Heat the oil in a flameproof casserole dish. Add onion, garlic and paprika and cook, stirring, 2 minutes. Add beef and cook 3 or 4 minutes, or until onion is soft and beef has browned. Add caraway seeds, bay leaves, vinegar and half of the stock. Season with salt and pepper and bring to a boil. Cover and simmer 1 hour.

Stir in remaining stock, potatoes, bell peppers, chilli, tomatoes and tomato paste.

Bring to a boil, reduce heat, cover and simmer 30 to 40 minutes, or until meat and vegetables are tender. Remove and discard bay leaves.

Braised Beef in Guinness

Slowly, slowly, slowly let the beef be braised
as Ireland's black magic pours:
May the Lord be praised!

Time to prepare – 10 minutes
Time to cook – 2 hours
Serves – 4

50g plain flour
Salt and freshly ground pepper
1 kilo of lean braising steak, trimmed and sliced thickly
4 tablespoons vegetable oil
3 large onions, sliced
1 tablespoon of brown sugar
600ml Guinness
Bouquet Garni sachet

Season the flour with salt and pepper and toss the meat in the mixture to coat.

Heat the oil in a large heavy pan and brown the meat in batches, and then set aside. Gently fry the onions in the same pan until soft, and then de-glaze the bottom of the pan with the Guinness and the sugar. Add the meat and bouquet garni. Bring to the boil. Reduce the heat, cover and cook very gently for about 2 hours until the meat is tender. Remove bouquet garni just before serving.

Curried Lamb with Raita

*Cucumber gentle
subcontinental.*

Time to prepare – 10 minutes
Time to cook – 50 minutes
Serves – 4

3 tablespoons olive oil
2 onions, finely chopped
1 piece fresh ginger – 1 cm,
peeled, grated
3 cloves garlic, crushed
1 teaspoon mild chilli powder
1^1/2 teaspoons turmeric
1^1/2 teaspoons ground
coriander
^{1}/2 teaspoon ground cumin
^{1}/2 teaspoon garam masala

450g lamb fillet, cubed
115ml plain yogurt
Salt and freshly ground black
pepper
Mint sprigs, to garnish

RAITA:
300ml plain yogurt
175g cucumber, diced
1 tablespoon chopped fresh
mint

Heat oil in a flameproof casserole dish. Add onions and cook,
stirring occasionally, 5 minutes, or until soft. Add ginger, garlic,
chilli powder, turmeric, coriander, cumin and garam masala and
cook, stirring, 2 minutes. Add lamb and cook, stirring, 2 minutes, or
until browned. Add yogurt, ^{1}/2 cup water, salt and pepper and stir
well. Bring to a boil, reduce heat and simmer 45 minutes.
Meanwhile, make Raita.

Mix together yogurt, cucumber and chopped mint. Season with
salt and pepper. Refrigerate until required. Garnish lamb with mint
sprigs and serve with raita.

Fruity Gammon Steaks

Time to prepare – 5 minutes
Time to cook – 20 minutes
Serves – 4

1 piece ginger ($^{1}/_{2}$-inch/1cm), peeled, grated
2 tablespoons tomato ketchup
1 tablespoon light brown sugar
1 tablespoon light soy sauce
1 tablespoon malt vinegar
1 tablespoon lemon juice
2 tablespoons olive oil
4 gammon steaks – 175g each
1 green bell pepper, chopped
1 red bell pepper, chopped
1 onion, chopped
1 can (8oz/225g) pineapple chunks, drained, with two
tablespoons juice reserved
1 tablespoon corn flour
Watercress, to garnish

In a bowl, mix together ginger, tomato ketchup, brown sugar, soy sauce, and vinegar and lemon juice. Set aside. Heat the oil in a flameproof casserole dish. Add gammon steaks and cook 5 minutes on each side.

Remove steaks from dish and keep warm. Add bell peppers and onion to dish and cook, stirring occasionally, 5 minutes, or until soft. Stir in ketchup mixture and pineapple chunks.

Blend reserved pineapple juice with corn flour. Add to dish and bring to a boil, stirring. Return steaks to dish and simmer 5 minutes. Garnish and serve.

Mediterranean Lamb

Time to prepare – 5 minutes + 30 minutes
Time to cook – 50 minutes
Serves – 4

1 aubergine, sliced
2 teaspoons salt
2 tablespoons olive oil, plus extra for brushing
450g lean lamb, cubed
2 leeks, sliced
1 green bell pepper, chopped
1 can (14oz/400g) chopped tomatoes
1 clove garlic, crushed
2 courgettes, sliced
1 tablespoon tomato purée or ketchup
1 tablespoon chopped fresh rosemary

Place the sliced aubergine in a colander, sprinkle with salt and let stand 30 minutes.

Preheat oven to 190c/gas 5. Heat the oil in a flameproof casserole dish. Add lamb and cook, stirring, 3 or 4 minutes, or until browned. Add leeks and cook, stirring, 4 or 5 minutes, or until soft. Stir in bell pepper, tomatoes, garlic, courgettes, tomato paste and rosemary. Simmer 5 – 10 minutes.

Rinse aubergine in cold water and pat dry with paper towels. Arrange aubergine slices on top of lamb mixture and brush with olive oil. Bake for 30 to 40 minutes, or until aubergine slices are golden brown and tender.

Serve hot.

Orange & Ginger Lamb

Time to prepare – 5 minutes + 2-3 hours marinating
Time to cook – 20 minutes
Serves – 4

2 tablespoons dark soy sauce
2 tablespoons dry sherry
1 tablespoon orange juice
2 cloves garlic, finely chopped
1 piece ginger ($^1/_2$-inch/1cm), peeled, grated
450g lean lamb, cut into strips
2 tablespoons vegetable oil
115g broccoli florets
225g carrots cut into matchsticks
1 red bell pepper, thinly sliced
1 teaspoon light brown sugar
Coriander sprigs, to garnish

In a bowl, mix together soy sauce, sherry, orange juice, garlic and ginger. Add the lamb and stir to coat with marinade and refrigerate 2 or 3 hours. Drain lamb, reserving marinade. Heat oil in a flameproof casserole dish. Add lamb and cook, stirring, 8 to 10 minutes, or until browned all over and cooked through. Add broccoli, carrots and bell pepper and cook, stirring, 5 minutes.

Pour in reserved marinade and sugar and bring to a boil. Reduce heat, cover and simmer 5 minutes. Garnish with coriander sprigs and serve immediately.

Pork Chops with a Cider Apple sauce

Time to prepare – 10 minutes
Time to cook – 75 minutes
Serves – 4

2 tablespoons olive oil
4 boneless (6oz/175g each) pork loin chops
450g onions, sliced
2 cloves garlic, crushed
12 plum tomatoes, peeled, chopped
150ml beef stock
55ml red-wine vinegar
700g crisp apples
2 tablespoons lemon juice
Salt and freshly ground black pepper

Preheat oven to gas 4 (180c). On the hob heat the olive oil in a
flameproof casserole dish. Add chops and cook 3 minutes on each
side, until browned.

Remove chops and keep warm. Add onions to dish and cook,
stirring occasionally, 5 minutes, or until soft. Add garlic and
tomatoes. Return chops to dish and pour in stock and red wine
vinegar. Bring to a boil. Meanwhile, peel apples and use a melon
baller to cut out ball-shaped pieces. Put apple balls into a bowl of
water with lemon juice, to prevent apple discolouring. Chop
remaining apple and add to dish. Cover and put in the oven for 1
hour.

Remove chops from dish and keep warm. Pour sauce into a
blender or food processor and process 1 minute. Season with salt
and pepper. Return to dish with chops and apple balls. Cook over
low heat 15 minutes, or until apple balls are just tender. Serve hot.

Harvest Casserole

Time to prepare – 10 minutes
Time to cook – 1^1/2 hours
Serves – 4

60ml olive oil	2 tablespoons plain flour
4 pork chops	300ml beef stock
1 large onion, sliced	300ml apple juice
2 leeks, chopped	Salt and freshly ground pepper
1 clove garlic, crushed	2 small apples
225g parsnips cut into chunks	175g self raising flour
225g carrots	1 teaspoon mixed dried herbs
1 teaspoon dried sage	85g vegetable or beef suet

Preheat oven to 170c/gas 4. Heat the oil in a large flameproof casserole dish. Add chops and cook 2 to 3 minutes on each side until browned. Remove from pan and drain on paper towels. Add onion, leeks and garlic and cook, stirring occasionally, 5 minutes, or until soft. Add parsnips, carrots and sage and cook 2 minutes. Add plain flour and cook, stirring, 1 minute. Gradually stir in stock and apple juice. Season with salt and pepper and bring to a boil. Replace chops, cover and bake 1^1/4 hours, or until pork is tender. Meanwhile, core and coarsely chop apples and set aside. Mix together self raising flour, herbs salt and pepper; cut in the suet. Add ^{3}/4 cup water and stir to a firm dough. Divide dough into 8 small dumplings. Stir apples into casserole. Place dumplings on top, return to oven and cook, uncovered, for 20 minutes. Serve immediately.

Herby Lamb Cobbler

Time to prepare – 10 minutes
Time to cook – 2^1/2 hours
Serves – 4

900g neck of lamb, boned, cubed
25g plain flour
1 tablespoon olive oil
1 large onion, chopped
55g dried peas, soaked overnight
225g carrots, diced
225g swede, diced
500ml chicken stock
Salt
Freshly ground black pepper
1 pinch (large) paprika

TOPPING:
225g plain flour
1^1/2 teaspoons baking powder
55g butter
1 teaspoon dried sage
1 egg
2 tablespoons milk, plus extra for brushing

Preheat oven to 160c/gas 4. Coat the lamb in flour. Heat the oil in a flameproof casserole dish. Add lamb and cook, stirring, until browned. Remove and set aside. Add onion and cook, stirring occasionally, 7 minutes, or until lightly browned. Return lamb and add peas, carrots and swede. Pour in stock and season with salt, pepper and paprika. Bring to a boil, cover and bake 2 hours. Sift flour, baking powder and salt into a bowl. Cut in butter until mixture resembles fine bread crumbs.

Stir in sage. Add egg and milk and stir to a soft dough. Knead on a lightly floured surface and roll out to ^{1}/2 inch thickness. Using a pastry cutter, cut out 1^1/2 inch round biscuits.

Arrange rounds on top of dish and brush with milk. Increase oven temperature to 200c/gas 6. Return dish to oven and cook, uncovered, 15 to 20 minutes, or until biscuits are risen and golden. Serve immediately.

Toad in the Hole

*Tell me, does your batter lack
Cumberland or Natterjack?*

Time to prepare – 5 minutes
Time to cook – 45 minutes
Serves – 4

115g plain flour
1 pinch salt
1 teaspoon mixed dried herbs
1 egg, beaten
300ml milk
1 tablespoon sunflower oil
1 small onion, chopped
450g sausages

Preheat oven to 200c/gas 6.

In a large bowl, mix together flour, salt and herbs. Make a well in centre and add egg and half of the milk. Beat to a smooth batter. Stir in remaining milk and mix until smooth.

Heat the oil in a shallow flameproof casserole dish. Add onion and cook, stirring occasionally, for about 3 minutes. Add sausages and cook until browned and cooked through. Drain off excess fat.

Pour batter into dish and bake 30 minutes, or until batter is risen and golden. Serve immediately.

Variation: There are many types of sausages available. Try using different types to vary this recipe.

Fillet steak with parsley mash and onion marmalade

Time to prepare – 10 minutes
Time to cook – 30 minutes
Serves – 4

1kg King Edward Potatoes	2 garlic cloves, crushed
125ml olive oil	2 tablespoons red wine vinegar
2 sprigs of rosemary	50g butter
4 tablespoons chopped fresh parsley	3 tablespoons milk
	A little nutmeg
3 onions, thinly sliced	4 x 175gm fillet steaks

Cut the potatoes into chunks and put into a pan of cold salted water and cook until tender. Meanwhile put 75ml olive oil and the rosemary into a small pan and gently heat and then set aside for 15 minutes. Remove the rosemary and discard. Add half the parsley and blitz with a hand blender or food processor and set aside. Heat the remaining oil in a frying pan, add the onions, garlic and cook over a low heat for about 20 minutes until softened. Add a pinch of sugar and the vinegar and cook for 7 minutes. Season to taste, remove from the heat and keep warm.

Drain the potatoes and then put back into the pan along with the butter, milk and nutmeg. Stir and add remaining parsley. Set aside and keep warm.

Heat a griddle pan until hot then cook the steaks for 4 minutes each side for medium.

To serve, make a small mound of potato in the centre of each plate, place the steak on top and a spoon of onion marmalade on top of the steak. Drizzle the rosemary oil around the potato and serve.

Veal with Mushrooms

Time to prepare – 10 minutes
Time to cook – 55 minutes
Serves – 4

    2 tablespoons olive oil
    4 slices bacon, cut into thin strips
    4 slices veal steaks – 225g each
    350g carrots -cut into thick strips
    4 plum tomatoes, peeled, quartered, seeded
    550ml beef stock
    115ml red wine
    450g mixed mushrooms
    55g butter, diced
    55g chopped fresh parsley

Heat the oil in a flameproof casserole dish. Add bacon and cook 3 or 4 minutes. Remove and drain on paper towels. Add veal and cook until browned on both sides.

Remove veal and drain on paper towels. Add carrots and tomatoes to dish and cook 2 or 3 minutes. Return veal to dish. Add stock and red wine. Bring to a boil, reduce heat, cover and simmer 40 minutes. Add mushrooms and bacon and cook 10 minutes, or until veal is tender.

Lift out veal and remove carrots, mushrooms and bacon with a slotted spoon. Keep warm. Strain sauce and return to pan. Bring to a boil and boil until reduced by one-third. Whisk in butter, a little at a time. Stir in parsley. Return bacon and vegetables to sauce and cook over low heat 2 minutes to warm through. Arrange veal on warmed serving plates, pour sauce over veal and serve.

VEGETARIAN

Fruits and roots and country cheeses,
the growing earth and food that pleases.

Notes

Leek and Cheese Tart

Time to prepare – 10 minutes
Time to cook – 30 minutes
Serves – 4

> 8 slim prepared leeks
> Salt and black pepper
> 250g ready made puff pastry
> 1 tablespoon french coarse grain mustard
> 1 egg
> 50g Lancashire cheese

Pre heat the oven to 230c/gas 7. Arrange the leeks in a frying pan, cover with water, add a pinch of salt and bring to the boil. Reduce the heat and simmer for about 6 minutes. While they are cooking, roll out the pastry to a 10 inch square and then put the pastry square onto a baking sheet. Cut a groove into the pastry about half an inch in from the outside edges. Drain the leeks and cool them under cold running water and then allow to dry. Put the leeks inside the groove of the pastry case and brush them with the mustard. Break the egg and beat it lightly and then brush around the outside edge of the tart. Grate the cheese and spread over the top of the leeks.

Bake in the oven for about 15 minutes or until the pastry has risen and the cheese has melted.

Serve hot or warm.

Mushroom & Nut Pilaf

Time to prepare – 10 minutes
Time to cook – 40 minutes
Serves – 4

45g butter
55g pine nuts
55g sunflower seeds
1 onion, chopped
2 leeks, chopped
1 red bell pepper, chopped
1 carrot, diced
225g Arborio rice
1 litre vegetable stock
115g button mushrooms, sliced
Salt
Freshly ground black pepper

Heat 1 tablespoon of butter in a flameproof casserole dish. Add pine nuts and sunflower seeds and cook until golden.

Remove seeds from dish with a slotted spoon and set aside. Heat the remaining butter in dish. Add onion, leeks, bell pepper and carrot and cook, stirring occasionally, 3 minutes. Add rice and cook, stirring, 2 minutes. Add stock, cover and bring to a boil. Simmer 30 minutes, or until most of liquid is absorbed and rice is just tender.

Add mushrooms, pine nuts and sunflower seeds and cook over low heat, stirring frequently, 10 minutes. Season with salt and pepper and serve.

Mushroom Gratin

Time to prepare – 5 minutes
Time to cook – 1¹/₂ hours
Serves – 4

15g butter
1 clove garlic, crushed
900g potatoes, thinly sliced
175g brown mushrooms, sliced
115g button mushrooms, sliced
Salt
Freshly ground black pepper
2 eggs, beaten
150ml milk
150ml crème fraiche
175g shredded Gruyere cheese
Chopped fresh parsley, to garnish

Preheat oven to 200c/gas 6. Grease the inside of an ovenproof dish with butter and garlic. Then put in half of the potatoes and mushrooms.

Top with remaining potatoes. Season generously with salt and pepper. Mix together eggs, milk and crème fraiche and pour over vegetables. Bake 1 hour.

Sprinkle cheese over top and bake for a further 25 minutes, or until cheese is melted and golden and vegetables are tender. Garnish with parsley and serve.

Oriental-Style Stuffed Peppers

The flavours of the Orient go well with baked peppers.

Time to prepare – 5 minutes
Time to cook – 60 minutes
Serves – 4

4 green or red bell peppers
175g Cooked white rice
2 teaspoons Oil
$^1/_4$ cup Onion, minced
1 teaspoon Ginger, fresh, peeled and minced
1 teaspoon Garlic, crushed
3 Tablespoons Soy sauce
1 Tablespoon Sherry
225ml veg stock

Cut the tops off the peppers. Remove the inner membrane. Drop into boiling water for 3 minutes. Drain. Heat the oil in a small frying pan. Add the onion, ginger and garlic. Cook for 2 minutes, stirring frequently. In a large bowl mix the rice, onion, ginger, garlic, soy, sherry and stock. Add the mixture to the peppers. Stand the peppers up in a deep casserole dish. Cover with foil and bake at 180c/gas 4 for 45 minutes. Remove the foil and bake for 15 minutes longer. Serve whilst hot.

Sun-Dried Tomato Risotto

Time to prepare – 5 minutes
Time to cook – 25 minutes
Serves – 2

   55g butter
   1 tablespoon olive oil
   2 red onions, chopped
   12 sun-dried tomatoes, chopped
   1 tablespoon pesto sauce
   225g Arborio rice
   1 litre vegetable stock
   225g mushrooms, sliced
   Salt
   Freshly ground pepper
   55g Parmesan cheese
   Chopped fresh flat-leaf parsley, to garnish

Heat butter and oil in a flameproof casserole dish. Add onions and cook, stirring occasionally, 5 minutes, or until soft.

Add sun-dried tomatoes and pesto sauce and cook 3 or 4 minutes. Add rice and cook, stirring, 1 minute. Stir in about one-third of stock and simmer, stirring occasionally, until most of liquid has been absorbed.

Stir in mushrooms and season with salt and pepper. Add half of the remaining stock and simmer, stirring occasionally. When most of liquid has been absorbed, stir in remaining stock and simmer until all liquid has been absorbed and rice is tender and creamy. Using a vegetable peeler, shave curls of fresh Parmesan cheese over risotto, sprinkle with parsley and serve.

Vegetable & Cheese Bake

Time to prepare – 10 minutes
Time to cook – 50 minutes
Serves – 4

6 slices wholemeal bread, thick sliced
2 courgettes, sliced
1 beefsteak tomato, chopped
175g mushrooms, chopped
400ml milk
5 eggs, beaten
1 tablespoon chopped fresh chives
Salt
Freshly ground black pepper
150g shredded cheddar cheese
Flat-leaf parsley sprigs, to garnish

Preheat oven to 200c/gas 6.

Cut the bread into strips. Arrange half of bread in a shallow ovenproof dish.

Spread courgettes, tomato and mushrooms over bread and top with remaining bread. In a large bowl, mix together milk and eggs. Add chives and season with salt and pepper.

Pour milk mixture over bread. Sprinkle cheese over top and bake 50 minutes, or until egg mixture has set and topping is golden brown. Garnish with flat-leaf parsley and serve immediately.

Vegetable Cobbler

A growing casserole courtyard
paved with cobble scones.

Time to prepare – 10 minutes
Time to cook – 50 minutes
Serves – 4

  1 tablespoon olive oil
  1 clove garlic, crushed
  2 leeks, thinly sliced
  2 teaspoons mustard seeds
  225g mushrooms, sliced
  225g broccoli florets
  175g fresh or frozen peas
  300ml single cream
  1 large pinch of freshly grated nutmeg
  1 teaspoon prepared English mustard
  1 tablespoon chopped fresh parsley
  200g puff pastry, thawed if frozen
  Milk for brushing

Heat the oil in a flameproof casserole dish. Add garlic and leeks and cook until soft. Add mustard seeds and cook until they start to pop. Add mushrooms, broccoli and peas. Cover and cook for 8 to 10 minutes, or until tender. Remove from heat. Stir in single cream, nutmeg, mustard and parsley. Preheat oven to 200c/gas 6.

Roll out pastry on a lightly floured surface. Using a pastry cutter, cut out twelve 2 inch rounds. Arrange on top of vegetable mixture. Brush with a little milk and bake 30 to 35 minutes, or until risen and golden. Serve hot.

Courgettes Gougere

Time to prepare – 5 minutes
Time to cook – 35 minutes
Serves – 4

2 tablespoons olive oil
5 courgettes, thinly sliced
300g button mushrooms
2 leeks, thinly sliced
2 teaspoons whole-grain mustard
300ml crème fraiche
Salt
Freshly ground black pepper

CHOUX PASTRY:
55g butter
225g plain flour
2 eggs, beaten

To make choux pastry, melt butter in $^2/_3$ cup water, then bring quickly to a boil. Remove from heat and immediately stir in flour. Beat well until mixture is smooth and comes away from sides of pan. Return to heat and cook over low heat, stirring, for 2 or 3 minutes. Remove from heat and gradually add eggs, beating well. Set aside. Preheat oven to 220c/gas 7 Heat the oil in a flameproof casserole dish. Add the courgettes, button mushrooms and leeks and cook, stirring occasionally, 6 to 8 minutes, or until tender.

Stir in mustard and crème fraiche and season with salt and pepper. Put choux pastry in a pastry bag fitted with a plain $^1/_2$-inch tip. Pipe small balls of pastry around edge of courgettes mixture. Bake for 20 to 30 minutes, or until pastry is risen and golden. Serve hot.

Stilton and Sage Farfalle

Time to prepare – 5 minutes
Time to cook – 12 minutes
Serves – 4

450g Farfalle – (although any pasta that you have will do)
1 garlic clove, crushed
150ml dry white wine
175g of stilton, crumbled
4 tablespoons thick plain greek yoghurt
4 fresh sage leaves, chopped
4 tablespoons freshly grated parmesan
Salt and freshly ground pepper to taste

Cook the pasta in boiling salted water for about 10 minutes or until al dente (slightly under done).

In a small saucepan, mix together the garlic and wine and cook over a high heat for 1 minute. Turn down the heat; add the stilton, greek yoghurt and sage to the pan. Heat gently, stirring constantly, until the cheese begins to melt. Drain the pasta and transfer to a warm serving bowl, pour the sauce over and toss thoroughly to combine.

Sprinkle the parmesan on top, a little seasoning and serve.

Vegetable and Potato Dishes

Those who sneer that Solanum's a dud
are deceived, and their name will be mud.
Spicy salads or fried,
they've not lived till they've tried
the stupendously versatile Spud.

Notes

Ye Olde Bubble and Squeak

This classic dish originally contained beef along with the left-over cooked potatoes and cabbage, though today people don't generally bother with the meat. The name is apparently due to the sounds that are emitted during cooking, the vegetables bubble as they are boiled and then squeak in the frying pan.

Time to prepare – 5 minutes
Time to cook – 20 minutes
Serves – 4

    25g Butter
    1 onion, finely chopped
    450g potatoes, cooked and mashed
    225g cabbage, finely chopped and cooked
    6 slices beef, cooked and finely chopped

Melt the butter in a large frying pan; add the onion and fry for a few minutes until softened, stirring frequently.

Add the potatoes and cabbage. If you are including the beef, add this as well. Fry over a medium heat for 15 minutes until brown then serve.

Serving hint: – fabulous for breakfast with chopped bacon instead of beef, with a fried egg on top.

Potato Mash with Garlic and Freshly Ground Black Pepper

Time to prepare – 5 minutes
Time to cook – 25 minutes
Serves – 4

> 500g King Edward potatoes,
> 100g Celeriac
> 1 clove garlic – crushed
> Freshly ground Black Pepper
> 25g unsalted butter
> 25g Parmesan cheese, freshly grated

Cut potatoes and celeriac into even-sized chunks and cook in salted water to cover until tender. Drain well, then mash smoothly. Beat in the unsalted butter, garlic, pepper and Parmesan. Season with salt and pepper to taste; and serve.

Smoked Cheese Scalloped Potatoes

Time to prepare – 5 minutes
Time to cook – 70 minutes
Serves – 4

> 3 large Potatoes, medium-thin sliced
> 100g Smoked Cheese, grated
> 2 tablespoons Onion, minced
> 1$^1/_2$ teaspoons Flour
> 500ml Milk
> Salt and pepper to taste

Heat oven to 190c/gas 5. Blanch potato slices in boiling water for 5 minutes. Drain and rinse with cold water. Lightly grease a casserole with oil. Make a layer of $^1/_2$ of the potatoes. Top with the cheese, onion, and flour. Top with the rest of the potatoes. Season slightly, heat the milk and pour over the casserole. Cover and bake for 50 minutes. Uncover and bake for 20 minutes longer (or until lightly brown).

Serve hot, but delicious cold.

Peter's Parsnip Purée

Time to prepare – 5 minutes
Time to cook – 30 minutes
Serves 4

750g Parsnips, peeled and roughly chopped
1 tablespoon double cream
25g butter
Salt and pepper
Curry powder – good pinch
1 egg, beaten
50g Dried breadcrumbs
3 tablespoons sunflower oil

Put the parsnips into a pan of cold water. Bring them to the boil and boil until tender, about 20-25 minutes depending on their size and age.

When they are soft, drain thoroughly and mash them to a soft pale yellow purée with the cream and butter, salt, pepper and curry powder.

Let the mixture cool, and then form it into little cakes about 5 cm (2 inches) across and 2.5 cm (1 inch) high.

Brush with beaten egg, dip into dried breadcrumbs and fry in the hot sunflower oil until golden on both sides.

Serve with almost anything!!! Except puddings of course!!

Creamed Parsnips

*This smooth purée is an excellent accompaniment to roast
meats, poultry and game. This was a popular dish in the
16th and 17th centuries, when food with a sweet flavour,
such as parsnips, was often served as a complement to savoury
dishes.*

Time to prepare – 5 minutes
Time to cook – 30-45 minutes
Serves – 4

900g parsnips – peeled and roughly chopped
150g single cream
Chopped fresh parsley – to garnish

Cook the parsnips in salted boiling water for 25-40 minutes, until
very tender.

Drain thoroughly then return to the pan and mash, using a
potato masher or a food processor.

Stir in the cream and season to taste. Heat gently, then serve hot,
garnished with parsley.

Italian Potato Bake

Time to prepare – 10 minutes
Time to cook – 60 minutes
Serves – 4

2 large red onions
1kg medium sized Potatoes
450g large red tomatoes – vine ripened are best
5 tablespoons olive oil
100g freshly grated Parmesan cheese
Fresh basil leaves – torn
5 tablespoons water
Salt and freshly ground pepper to taste

Preheat the oven to 180c/gas 4

Brush a baking dish with oil and then just wipe the clove of garlic over the oiled surface.

Spread a layer of the onions on the bottom of the dish and then a layer of overlapping potato and tomato slices and season. Sprinkle a little oil and a little cheese over. Then another layer of onions followed by another layer of overlapping slices of potato and tomatoes. Pour the water over and then scatter the torn basil leaves over. Now sprinkle the remainder of the oil and Parmesan cheese over the top and put into the oven for about an hour.

Then serve whilst still hot

English Mustard Mash

O to be in England
with the wisdom of a child!
O to be in England
where the Mustard Mash grows wild!

Time to prepare – 5 minutes
Time to cook – 20 minutes
Serves – 4

> 8 large potatoes, peeled and cut into even chunks
> 250ml full cream milk
> 75g unsalted butter
> 4 tablespoons English mustard
> Salt and freshly ground pepper to taste

Put the potatoes into a large saucepan, cover with cold salted water and bring to the boil. Simmer gently for 15 minutes or until tender. Remove from the pan and drain. Put the milk and butter into the empty pan, heat to melt the butter and bring to the boil. Return the potatoes to the pan and mash thoroughly. Add the mustard and mix well, season to taste.

Wonderful with sausages for a delicious variation on Bangers and Mash!

Irish-Style Onion Rings

I will arise and go now, and go for onion rings . . .
and feast alone where my table's laid.

Time to prepare – 5 minutes
Time to cook – 10 minutes
Serves – 4

200g Cream Cracker crumbs
$1/2$ teaspoon Garlic powder
$1/2$ teaspoon Onion powder
$1/8$ teaspoon Pepper
225ml Guinness (You can use any beer in this recipe, but Guinness works best)
1 Egg
150g Flour
2 large Onions
Oil for frying

Mix together the crumbs, garlic powder, onion powder and pepper. Lightly beat the egg in a separate bowl. Whisk in the flour and beer. Slice the onions into $1/4$-inch rings. Preheat the oil to 360c. Dip the rings first into the batter and then into the crumbs. Add to the hot oil in batches (turning once) and cook until lightly brown (about 2 minutes). Drain on paper towels.

PUDDINGS

Don't desert dessert, my friend –
the flower's only budding;
no, don't desert dessert, my friend –
our meal must end with pudding!

Gran's Baked Apples in Batter

*A dappled apple
in a better batter.*

Time to prepare – 10 minutes
Time to cook – 50 minutes
Serves – 4

>2 tablespoons golden syrup
>4 sweet apples, cored
>8 bay leaves
>Icing sugar for dusting

BATTER:
>55g plain flour
>2 eggs, beaten
>1 teaspoon vanilla extract
>300ml milk
>55g sugar
>15g butter, melted

Preheat oven to 190c/gas 5. Lightly butter an ovenproof dish and spread golden syrup over the bottom of the dish.

Place apples on top of the syrup. Put a bay leaf in cavity of each apple, reserving 4 remaining leaves for decoration. Bake for 15 minutes. Meanwhile, make batter. Sift flour into a large bowl and make a well in centre. Add eggs, vanilla extract and a little milk. Beat into flour, gradually adding more milk to form a smooth batter. Stir in sugar and melted butter. Pour batter over apples and bake 45 to 50 minutes, or until batter is risen and golden. Remove bay leaves from apples. Decorate with reserved bay leaves, dust with icing sugar and serve.

Baked Panettone Pudding

Time to prepare – 5 minutes plus 15 minutes soaking
Time to cook – 50 minutes
Serves – 2

    2 eggs, beaten
    75g sugar
    200ml whole milk
    $^1/_2$ teaspoon vanilla extract
    3 slices panettone with dried fruit -or other rich yeast bread
    1 tablespoon marmalade
    Icing sugar for dusting

In a large bowl, beat eggs and sugar until light and foamy. Add milk and vanilla extract and mix well.

Lightly butter a shallow ovenproof dish. Spread slices of panettone with orange marmalade. Sandwich together, 2 pieces at a time, and cut the pieces in half. Arrange in a dish. Ladle the egg mixture over the panettone and soak 15 minutes.

Preheat oven to 165c/gas 3. Place dish in a larger ovenproof dish or roasting pan and pour in enough boiling water to come halfway up the sides of dish. Bake 50 minutes, or until custard is set and top is golden with a slight crust. Sprinkle with icing sugar and serve hot or cold.

Coffee Brulee

*Cappuccino, ***** or latte,*
summer fruits and a coffee brulee.

Time to prepare – 5 minutes
Time to cook – 45 minutes
Serves – 4

   8 egg yolks
   115g sugar
   250ml whole milk
   500ml whipping cream
   1 teaspoon coffee extract
   Summer berries, to decorate

TOPPING:
   55g sugar

In a large bowl, beat together egg yolks and sugar until light and
foamy. Put milk, cream and coffee flavouring in a flameproof
casserole dish. Simmer but do not boil. Remove from heat and let
cool. Preheat oven to 130c/gas 2. Pour milk mixture into egg yolk
mixture and stir well. Pour into a measuring jug and allow froth to
rise to surface. Skim off froth. Pour mixture back into dish.

   Put a piece of greaseproof paper in a roasting pan. Put dish on top
of the paper. Pour enough boiling water into pan to come halfway
up side of dish. Bake 45 minutes, or until mixture has set. Let cool,
then refrigerate.

   To make topping, preheat grill until very hot. Sprinkle top of
custard with sugar and grill until sugar melts and turns a deep
golden brown. Decorate with summer berries and serve.

Flambéed Fruit

Impetuous and passionate the game
when the spirits of the evening are aflame . . .

Time to prepare – 5 minutes
Time to cook – 10 minutes
Serves – 4

    55g butter
    55g sugar
    2 oranges, peeled, segmented
    1 cans (12oz/350g) pineapple pieces in natural juice
    4 bananas, thickly sliced
    1 tablespoon orange liqueur or brandy
    Mint sprigs, to garnish

Put butter and sugar in a flameproof casserole dish and cook over low heat until melted and a caramel colour.

Add oranges, pineapple chunks and their juice and bananas. Bring to a boil and boil 5 minutes, or until sauce thickens.

Put liqueur or brandy in a ladle and warm gently. Set alight and pour over fruit. Cook 1 minute, until flames die down. Garnish with mint and serve warm.

Classic Queen of Puddings

Meringue, Your Majesty?

Time to prepare – 10 minutes
Time to cook – 50 minutes
Serves – 4

500 ml milk
55g butter
115g cake crumbs
Grated rind of 1 orange
Grated rind of 1 lemon
55g sugar
4 egg yolks, beaten
2 egg whites, beaten until stiff

55g strawberry jam
115g strawberries, sliced
Icing sugar for dusting

MERINGUE:
2 egg whites
60g sugar

Preheat oven to 170c/gas 4.

Put milk and butter into a flameproof casserole dish and heat gently
until butter melts. Stir in cake crumbs and lemon and orange rinds.
Whisk in sugar and egg yolks. Fold in the egg whites. Put the dish in
a deep roasting pan and pour in enough boiling water to come
halfway up side of dish. Bake for 45 to 50 minutes or until set. Mix
together jam and strawberries and spread over top of pudding.
Remove pudding from water. To make meringue, beat egg whites
until they form stiff peaks. Beat in the sugar.

Put mixture in a pastry bag with a star tip and pipe in a lattice
pattern on top of pudding. Dust with icing sugar and bake 30
minutes. Serve warm.

Rhubarb Meringue

Time to prepare – 5 minutes
Time to cook – 40 minutes
Serves – 4

450g rhubarb, sliced
4 bananas, sliced
55g light-brown sugar
5g ground cinnamon
Grated rind of 3 oranges
Juice of 3 oranges

MERINGUE:
3 egg whites
175g sugar

Preheat oven to 180c/gas 4. Put rhubarb and bananas in an ovenproof dish. Sprinkle with brown sugar, cinnamon and orange rind. Add orange juice, making sure fruit is evenly coated.

Cover with a lid or piece of foil and bake 15 to 20 minutes, or until fruit is tender. Meanwhile, to make meringue, beat egg whites until they form stiff peaks. Beat in sugar.

Put meringue into a pastry bag with a star tip and pipe over fruit. Return to oven and cook 20 minutes, or until meringue is crisp and golden. Serve warm or cold.

Rice Pudding with Peaches

Time to prepare – 5 minutes
Time to cook – 50 minutes
Serves – 4

850ml whole milk
6 cardamom pods
115g short-grain rice
55g pistachios, chopped
115g packed light-brown sugar
55g butter, diced
2 egg yolks
1 can (14oz/400g) peach halves, drained

Pour milk into a flameproof casserole dish. Add cardamom pods, bring to a boil, reduce heat and simmer 5 minutes. Remove cardamom pods. Stir in rice.

Return to a boil, reduce heat and simmer, stirring frequently, 15 to 20 minutes, or until rice is tender and most of liquid has been absorbed. Remove from heat and stir in pistachio nuts, half of the brown sugar, butter and egg yolks. Let cool slightly. Preheat oven to 170c/gas 3

Remove half of mixture from dish and set aside. Arrange peaches on top of rice in dish and cover with remaining rice. Bake 25 minutes. Preheat griller. Sprinkle pudding with remaining sugar and grill until sugar melts and turns a deep golden brown. Serve warm.

Saucy Lime Pie

Time to prepare – 5 minutes
Time to cook – 40-50 minutes
Serves – 4

> 55g unsalted butter, softened
> 55g sugar
> Grated rind of 3 limes
> Juice of 3 limes
> 2 eggs, separated
> 55g self raising flour
> 300ml milk

Preheat oven to gas 4 (160c). In a large bowl, beat together butter, sugar and lime rind until light and fluffy. Stir in egg yolks and carefully fold in flour. Stir in milk and lime juice.

Whisk egg whites until they form stiff peaks. Fold into lime mixture. Lightly butter an ovenproof dish.

Pour lime mixture into dish and bake 40 to 50 minutes, or until risen and golden. Serve warm.

Makes 4 servings.

Ignorance is Bliss

Folly to be wise? I doubt it.
Just believe your eyes – then shout it!

Time to prepare – 5 minutes + chilling
Serves – 4

1 pint Whipping Cream
A good splash of Baileys, Amerula, Tia Maria, or favourite liqueur
1 Crunchie – smashed with a rolling pin whilst still in packet

Whisk together the cream and liqueur until almost firm then add Crunchie pieces and whisk for 15 seconds. Leave to chill in fridge for 1 hour minimum.

Just the simplest thing to make, but tastes out of this world!!

Notes

Mint White Chocolate Mousse

Time to prepare – 10 minutes + chilling
Serves – 4

   4oz Chocolate, white
   3 tablespoons Crème de menthe, green
   $^1/_4$ pint double cream,
   2 Egg whites (at room temperature)

Melt the white chocolate in a double boiler, or a glass bowl sat on a pan of boiling water. When melted, stir in the crème de menthe. Let it cool a bit and stir in about $2^1/_2$ tablespoons of cream. Leave to cool.

Beat the egg whites until stiff, but not dry. Fold the chocolate-crème-cream mixture into the beaten egg whites. The more carefully you fold; the lighter will be the mousse.

Whip the remaining cream, until soft peaks form. Fold the egg whites-chocolate mixture into the whipped cream. Again, the more air you preserve, the lighter the mousse. Spoon carefully into small bowls or cups and chill for about two hours.

Serve topped with a strawberry.

Tipsy Fruit Fool

Apricot brandy's the pool
in which splashes this Tipsy Fruit Fool.

Time to prepare – 5 minutes
Time to cook – 10 minutes + chilling
Serves – 4

> 500g cooking apples, peeled, sliced
> 155g dried apricots, pre-soaked
> 60g icing sugar
> rind of 3 satsumas
> juice of 3 satsumas
> 30ml apricot brandy
> 90ml fromage frais
> chocolate curls to decorate

In a saucepan, combine apples, apricots, sugar and satsuma rind and juice. Bring to a boil.

Cover and cook until apples and apricots are tender. Remove satsuma rind and reserve some for decoration. Let stand until cold.

In a food processor fitted with a metal blade, process apple mixture to a purée.

Add apricot brandy and fromage frais and process until well blended. Divide mixture among individual glasses and chill until needed.

Using a sharp knife, cut reserved rind in thin strips. Decorate desserts with satsuma rind strips and chocolate curls.

Spicy French Toast

Time to prepare – 15 mins
Time to cook – 10 mins
Serves – 4

  4 slices of white bread
  3 large eggs
  1 teaspoon grated nutmeg
  1 teaspoon cinnamon
  A little caster sugar
  4 tablespoons of double cream

Cut the crusts off the bread and cut into triangles, beat the eggs with the grated nutmeg and cinnamon. Heat a frying pan with a little oil and butter in it. Dip each piece of bread into the egg mixture and fry until golden brown before turning and cook on the other side.

To serve put 4 triangles onto each plate, sprinkle with a little cinnamon and caster sugar, and serve warm with a dollop of double cream.

Chocolate Fruit Pudding

Time to prepare – 15 minutes
Time to cook – 2 hours
Serves – 6

200g wholemeal bread without crusts
150ml water
3 tablespoons skimmed milk
Few drops of vanilla essence
200g porridge oats
75g light brown sugar
2 teaspoons mixed spice
$1^1/2$ teaspoons of baking powder
Pinch of salt
75g Flora margarine or similar
225g mixed dried fruit
2 tablespoons sifted cocoa powder

Break the bread into small pieces, place into a large bowl. Mix the cold water, milk and vanilla essence together and pour over the bread and leave to soak for 15 minutes, and then beat until smooth. In another bowl, mix together the oats, sugar, cocoa, mixed spice, baking powder and salt together and then add to the smooth bread mixture. Melt the margarine and stir into the mixture. Add the fruit and mix thoroughly.

Place the mixture into a greased 2 litre basin, cover with greased grease proof paper and steam for $1^1/2 – 1^3/4$ hours. Serve with real custard.

Banana and Mango Fool

Time to prepare – 5 minutes + chilling
Serves – 4

   4 small bananas, peeled and sliced
   1 ripe mango, peeled and chopped
   Grated zest and juice of one lime
   2 tablespoons caster sugar
   300ml double cream

Purée the bananas, mango, lime juice and sugar together in a blender. Whip the cream until it stands in soft peaks, and then gently fold into the mango mixture a little at a time. Put into glass dishes and chill until required.

   When ready to eat, sprinkle with grated lime zest and serve.

Notes

Hot Peaches with Honey and Mascarpone

Time to prepare – 10 minutes
Time to cook – 5 minutes
Serves – 4

4 fresh peaches
100g Marscapone cheese
3 tablespoons clear honey
2 tablespoons flaked almonds

For the syrup
200g sugar
400ml of water
Half a teaspoon vanilla essence
Juice of half a lemon

First of all make the syrup. Gently dissolve the sugar in the water in the pan. Add the essence and lemon juice. Half the peaches, remove the stones, add to the syrup and poach for 4 minutes or until soft. To serve, fill each peach with Marscapone, drizzle with honey and sprinkle with flaked almonds.

Banana and Coconut Crème Brulee

Time to prepare – 5 minutes
Time to cook – 30 minutes
Serves – 4

568ml double cream
75g Coconut Milk Powder (or 3 fl. oz. Coconut cream)
4 eggs yolks, size 3
40g caster sugar
1 small banana

To serve: – 100g soft brown sugar
A little icing sugar for dusting the plate

Preheat the oven 150c/gas 2

In a small saucepan, heat the cream until it is almost boiling, then add the coconut milk and combine with a whisk.
In a glass bowl beat the caster sugar and eggs yolks together until they look pale, and then pour the hot cream into the egg mixture, stirring all the time.
Put two or three pieces of sliced banana onto the bottom of the ramekin dishes and then gently pour the custard into the dishes until almost full.
Place the dishes into a roasting tin, and then pour water into the tin until it comes about halfway up the ramekins
Bake for 25 minutes until the top is set.
Sprinkle the brown sugar over the tops and either place under a grill, or by using a blow torch, heat until the sugar melts and caramelizes.

Proper Custard

Time to prepare – 5 minutes
Time to cook – 15 minutes
Serves – 4

300ml full cream milk
300ml double cream
4 egg yolks
2 tablespoons caster sugar
1 vanilla pod, split
1 tablespoon of water
1 tablespoon of cornflour

Gently warm the cream and milk in a saucepan with the vanilla pod but do not let it boil. Beat the egg yolks with the sugar, remove the vanilla pod from the cream mixture and pour slowly onto the eggs, stirring constantly. Mix the cornflour with the water and pour into the egg mixture. Return the mixture to the saucepan and stir over a low heat until the mixture thickens and coats the back of a spoon (about 10 minutes). Again, do not allow to boil. Strain the custard into a bowl and put a piece of damp cling film on the surface to prevent a skin forming and chill.

KIDS' CORNER

Traffic Lights

Makes 4

1 packet chocolate instant milk pudding
1 packet banana instant milk pudding
1 packet strawberry instant milk pudding
3 x 268ml milk

Make up chocolate pudding as directed on packet and pour into the bottom of four glass or plastic tumblers.
Repeat with the banana mix and pour on top.
Finally repeat with the strawberry mix, and there you are, traffic lights!!!!!.
Chill until needed

The Easiest Oatmeal Chocolate Cookies

2 cups of caster sugar
25g of margarine
50ml full cream milk
1 teaspoon of Vanilla extract
2 tablespoons of Peanut Butter
2 tablespoons of Cocoa
3 cups porridge oats

Mix the first three ingredients in saucepan. Boil for one minute. Remove from the heat. Add the remaining ingredients. Scoop and drop by tablespoon onto greaseproof paper and cool.   That's all folks!!

Giant Banana Delight

3 bananas, peeled and cut into chunks
4 scoops of vanilla ice cream
fudge ice cream topping
4 scoops of strawberry ice cream

Strawberry ice cream topping
   can spray whipped cream
   a few nuts for topping
   Glacee cherries

Put half of the banana chunks in a glass bowl. Put the scoops of vanilla ice cream on top of the bananas. Squeeze the fudge topping over the ice cream. Top with the remaining banana chunks and scoops of strawberry ice cream. Use a spoon to drizzle the strawberry topping over ice cream. Squirt the whipped cream over the ice cream. Sprinkle with nut topping. Top with cherries. Serve right away. Makes 4 servings

Pop Pudding Chillers

$^1/_2$ pint of cold milk
1 packet instant milk pudding – any flavour
Six 5 ounce paper cups

Pour the milk into medium bowl. Add the mix. Whisk for 2 minutes. Spoon into cups. Insert wooden pop stick into each for a handle. Freeze overnight until firm. To remove the pop from cup, place the bottom of cup under warm running water for 15 seconds. Press firmly on the bottom of cup to release pop. (DO NOT TWIST OR PULL STICK). Makes 6 pops.

Nutty Nests

4 tablespoons of peanut butter
1 tablespoon of honey
2$^1/_2$ teaspoons of powdered milk
1-3 tbsp. porridge oats
Chinese noodles
Sugar covered almonds

Mix first 4 ingredients together in a bowl with a spoon. Then form into balls and make a "nest" in the centre with a spoon or your thumb. Add the Chinese noodles for "twigs" and the sugar covered almonds for "eggs". Makes 3-4 nests.

Creepy Crispy Caterpillar

3 tablespoons of margarine or butter
1 packet miniature marshmallows
6 yoghurt pots of Rice Krispies cereal
Prepared icing for decoration

In a large microwave-safe bowl, heat margarine and marshmallows at HIGH for 3 minutes, stirring after 2 minutes. Stir in rice Krispies until well coated. Using spatula sprayed with a little cooking spray oil, press mixture into a 15 x 10 x 1-inch pan coated with a little butter or oil. Allow mixture to cool slightly. Make caterpillar sections, using a small round cookie cutter, cut cereal mixture into circles. Place eight to nine sections next to each other to form caterpillar. Decorate with icing to make antenna, eyes, feet and spots on caterpillars.

S' mores (as featured on Barney!!!)

Cream Crackers
Marshmallows
Any plain chocolate bar cut into pieces

Place a square of chocolate onto cream cracker. Place marshmallow on top of chocolate. Place another piece of chocolate on top of marshmallow and top with another cream cracker. Microwave on medium until marshmallow begins to *grow*. Do not over cook. The warm marshmallow will melt the chocolate when squished together.

Index

2 a.m.French Onion Soup   16

Baby Leaf Salad with Wild Mushrooms and Chicken   23
Baked Cod Itallienne   45
Baked Panettone Pudding   107
Baked Saddle of Salmon   41
Banana and Coconut Crème Brulee   121
Banana and Mango Fool   119
Beef goulash with Chilli   70
Braised Beef In Guinness   71
Brie and Spiced Pear Tartlets   26
Broccoli & Cheese Soup   13

Chicken and Fruit Salad with a Mango Vinaigrette   36
Chicken Breast stuffed with Palma Ham & Mozzarella   56
Chicken Livers with Mango   59
Chicken on the vine   58
Chocolate Fruit Pudding   118
Classic Queen of Puddings   110
Coffee Brulee   108
Courgette Gougere   92
Creamy Wild Mushrooms in a Rich White Sauce   34
Creepy Crispy Caterpillar   126
Cucumber, Dill and Cheese Mousse   30
Curried Lamb with Raita   72

Duck Breasts with Apples and Prunes   54

Easy Peasy Spanish Omelette   22
English Mustard Mash   103

Fillet Steak with Parsley Mash And Onion Marmalade 80
Fillets of Sole with Mint & Cucumber 50
Fish Gratins 47
Fishy Parcels 32
Flambeed Fruit 109
Fruity Gammon Steaks 73

Garlic Roasted Chicken 55
Giant Banana Delight 125
Grans Baked Apples in Batter 106

Halibut with a Rich Orange Sauce 42
Harvest Casserole 77
Herby Lamb Cobbler 78
Hot Peaches with Honey and Mascarpone 120

Ignorance is Bliss 114
Irish Style Onion Rings 104
Is it a Pizza or is it an Omelette? 24
Italian Potato Bake 100

King Prawns in Pernod with a Creamy Tarragon Sauce 33

Latvian Potato Pancakes with Smoked Salmon 37
Leek and Cheese Tart 85
Lemon Chicken Couscous 64

Mediterranean Lamb 74
Mint White Chocolate Mousse 115
Monkfish on Ratatouille 48

Mushroom and Nut Pilaf	86
Mushroom Gratin	87
Mussels in White Wine	27
Nutty Nests	126
Orange and Ginger Lamb	75
Orchard Chicken	53
Oriental Style Stuffed Peppers	88
Pear and Watercress Soup with Blue Cheese Croutons	18
Peters Parsnip Purée	102
Peter's Perfect Parsnips	101
Pop Pudding Chillers	125
Pork Chops with a Cider Apple Sauce	76
Potato Mash with Garlic and Freshly Ground Pepper	98
Proper Custard	122
Ragout of Chicken with wild Mushrooms	57
Rhubarb Meringue	111
Rice Pudding with Peaches	112
Roast Parsnip Soup	15
Saucy Lime Pudding	113
Scampi Olé	46
Sea Queen Scallops with Lemon	43
Seafood Lasagne	44
Seafood Souffle Omelette	25
Smoked Cheese Scalloped Potatoes	99
Smoked Salmon and Prawn Gateaux with Chive Oil	28
S'mores	127
Spicy French Toast	117
Stilton and Sage Farfalle	93

Stilton and Walnut salad   21
Stuffed British Poussin with a Watercress sauce   60
Sun Dried Tomato Risotto   89

Tarragon Stuffed Mushrooms   35
Thai Chicken   62
The Big Chefs Hot Pot   69
The Easiest Oatmeal Chocolate Cookies   124
Tipsy Fruit Fool   116
Toad in the hole   79
Tomato and Red Pepper Soup and quick   17
Traffic Lights   124
Turkey Milanese   63
Tuscan Bean Soup   14

Veal with Mushrooms   81
Vegetable and Cheese Bake   90
Vegetable Cobbler   91

Ye Olde Bubble and Squeak   97